Eat Green

Jean Feldman and Holly Karapetkova

Tune: Jenny Jenkins

www.rourkeclassroom.com

Will you eat green,

Oh my children dear,

Will you eat green my children?

Oh, we'll eat green

Spinach, broccoli, and beans.

Veggie-weggie, fruity-tooty,

Fresh foody, colors of the rainbow.

Let's all eat green.

Will you eat orange,

My children dear,

Will you eat orange my children?

Oh, we'll eat orange things

Carrots, peaches, tangerines.

Veggie-weggie, fruity-tooty,

Fresh foody, colors of the rainbow.

Let's all eat orange.

Will you eat yellow,

My children dear,

Will you eat yellow my children?

Oh, we'll eat yellow corn,

Squash, pineapples, and more.

Veggie-weggie, fruity-tooty,

Fresh foody, colors of the rainbow.

Let's all eat yellow.

Will you eat red,

Oh my children dear,

Will you eat red my children?

Oh, red we'll eat

Apples, strawberries, and beets.

Veggie-weggie, fruity-tooty,

Fresh foody, colors of the rainbow.

Let's all eat red.

Will you eat blue and purple,

My children dear,

Will you eat blue and purple?

Oh, we'll eat purple, blue

Grapes, plums, and berries too.

Veggie-weggie, fruity-tooty,

Fresh foody, colors of the rainbow.

Let's all eat purple and blue.

Oh what will you eat, my children dear,
Oh what will you eat, my children?
Oh, we'll eat fresh foods
Good for us and the Earth, too.

Veggie-weggie, fruity-tooty,
Fresh foody, colors of the rainbow.
Let's all eat green.